Little Book of Druid Invocations and Charms

Handbook for Wheel of the Year Celebrations

Lily Ennis

Cover by Get Covers.

Contents

Introduction

The turning of the Wheel of the Year is a sacred dance, a rhythm that pulses through the land, the sky, and the depths of our souls. Since ancient times, Druids have honored the cycles of nature, embracing the wisdom of the seasons, the power of the elements, and the presence of the unseen forces that weave through all existence. Through invocation, we call upon these energies—gods and goddesses, ancestors and spirits, the essence of earth, air, fire, and water—to guide us, bless us, and walk beside us on our spiritual path.

This book is a collection of invocations crafted to enhance and deepen your connection to the eight great festivals of the Druidic tradition: the Winter Solstice, Imbolc, the Spring Equinox, Beltane, the Summer Solstice, Lughnasadh, the Autumn Equinox, and Samhain. Whether you are standing beneath the dark midwinter sky, kindling the fires of Beltane, or welcoming the harvest's bounty, these sacred words will help you attune to the spirit of the moment and commune with the forces of nature.

Each invocation is designed to be spoken aloud alone or in a gathered circle. It invokes the presence of the divine and the blessings of the land. Invocations are offerings of reverence, gratitude, and intention—words infused with the power of the old ways and the timeless wisdom of Druidry.

I wrote this book as a companion to *Druidry: A Timeless Path of Wisdom, Nature, and Spirituality*, in which many imagined invocations, charms and prayers used in Druid ceremonies are included. *The Little Book of Druid Invocations and Charms* includes dozens of additional prayers as well as how you might lay out your ritual space for each ceremony. It is designed as a quick reference that can be quickly sourced during your ritual.

May these invocations serve as a bridge between you and the sacred. May they awaken the deep knowing within you and root you firmly in the ancestors' path. And may the spirits of the earth, sea, and sky bless you as you walk in harmony with the Wheel of the Year.

Blessed be and may the light of wisdom guide your journey.

Chapter One

Winter Solstice: A Season of Renewal

The Winter Solstice, known in Druidry as Alban Arthan, or "The Light of Arthur," signifies a time of profound stillness and renewal. It marks the longest night and the shortest day of the year, a liminal moment when darkness peaks; yet the promise of returning light lies within it. For Druids, this is a sacred time of reflection, transformation, and rebirth, as the sun, having journeyed to its lowest point, begins its ascent once more, heralding the slow return of warmth and life to the land.

In the Druidic tradition, the Winter Solstice is deeply symbolic of the eternal cycle of death and rebirth. It is a time when the Great Mother gives birth to the Mabon, the Child of Light, who will grow in strength as the days lengthen. This story echoes through many mythological traditions, where a solar deity is born from the depths of darkness, ensuring the renewal of life. The Oak King, representing the waxing year, is said to triumph over the Holly King, who rules the waning half of the year, signaling the return of vitality and hope.

Druids honor this sacred time by gathering to witness the first rays of the returning sun, often at ancient sites aligned with the solstice, such as Newgrange in Ireland or Stonehenge in England. Rituals may include lighting candles or fires to symbolize the sun's rebirth, offering prayers of gratitude, and reflecting on the past year's lessons. It is a time to release what no longer serves us, embrace the stillness of winter, and set intentions for the growing light ahead.

Alban Arthan reminds us that even in our darkest moments, the spark of renewal is always present, waiting to emerge and illuminate our path once more.

Preparing the Ritual Space

Preparing a ritual space for the Druid ceremony of Alban Arthan, involves creating an environment that honors the season's themes of darkness, rebirth, and renewal. The space is ideally set in nature, such as within a grove of evergreen trees or a stone circle, but if held indoors, it should be decorated to evoke the sacred connection with the land.

The preparation begins by cleansing the area, often through smudging with sacred herbs like sage or cedar, sprinkling water from a blessed source, or using sound, such as a bell or chanting, to purify the space. An altar is arranged at the center or focal point of the ritual area, adorned with symbols of the solstice—evergreens representing resilience, holly and mistletoe for protection and fertility, and a Yule log or candle to symbolize the return of the sun's light.

The four directions may be acknowledged with corresponding elements: a bowl of water in the west, a candle or small fire in the south, a feather or incense in the east, and a stone or soil in the north. Participants may form a circle around the altar, marking the boundary with natural objects such as stones, branches, or lanterns to define the sacred space. As darkness falls, the ritual space is illuminated with lanterns, candles, or a central fire, emphasizing the journey from the longest night back into the growing light.

Before the ceremony begins, moments of quiet reflection or meditation allow participants to attune themselves to the energies of the season, ensuring that the space is not only physically prepared but also spiritually charged for the solstice celebration.

The following invocations can be spoken alone or as part of a ritual to honor the Winter Solstice.

Invocation to the Returning Sun

"O Great Wheel, turn once more!
From deepest night, the light is reborn.
Golden Child of the sky, rise anew,
Your fire kindles hope in the heart of the land.
Bless us with your radiant glow,
Guide us through the dark to the dawn beyond.
Hail the Sun, the light of life."

Blessing of the Bonfire

"Sacred flame, bright and bold,
Guardian of warmth in winter's hold,
With your flickering tongues, we call forth light,
To banish the dark and embrace the night.
May your embers carry our prayers on high,
As the old year fades and the new draws nigh.
We honor the fire, the heart of the Solstice."

Offering of the Evergreen Boughs

"O spirits of Yew, of Pine, of Fir,
Ancient ones who never wither nor fade,
In you, the promise of life endures,
Through winter's chill and summer's blaze.
Bless this home, bless this hearth,
With strength unyielding and wisdom vast.
We offer these boughs in sacred trust."

Invocation of the Holly and Ivy

"Holly bright, with crimson bead,
Ivy green, on stone you weave,
Sacred twins of frost and flame,
Woven deep in nature's name.
Holly, warder, guardian true,
Ivy, binder, ever new,
Balance held 'twixt dark and light,
Bless us on this Solstice night."

Invocation of the Spiced Fruits

"Blessed be the fruit of earth,
Sun-born gifts of golden worth.
Apple, sacred, wise and sweet,
Orange bright with spice and heat.
By clove and rind, by zest and seed,
Bring forth joy, fulfill our need.
With every bite, we honor thee,
Nature's bounty, wild and free."

Calling to the Spirits of Winter

"O Spirits of Frost, of Ice, of Storm,

Ancient wanderers of the northern wind,
We honor your wisdom, your stillness, your song.
Teach us patience in the hush of snow,
Teach us endurance as the cold winds blow.
But let the promise of light remain,
A seed of warmth in the dark domain.
With reverence, we call to thee."

Chapter Two

Spring Equinox: The Balance of Light and Dark

A Druid spring equinox ceremony celebrates the balance of light and dark, marking the transition from winter to spring. This time represents renewal, fertility, and gratitude for the Earth's awakening after the colder months. While practices vary among Druidic groups, the ceremony typically includes symbolic actions, meditations, and invocations that honor the cycle of nature.

Preparation

Preparing a ritual space for the Druid ceremony of the Spring Equinox, or Alban Eilir, involves creating a sacred environment that reflects the balance of light and dark and the renewal and fertility of the season. Ideally, the space is set in a natural location, such as a meadow, near a flowing stream, or within a grove where the signs of spring's awakening—budding trees, emerging flowers, and the songs of returning birds—can be observed. If held indoors, the space can be adorned with symbols of new life, including fresh flowers, eggs, and seeds, to honor the earth's renewal.

The preparation begins with cleansing the area, gently sweeping, sprinkling water collected from a natural source, or burning incense such as lavender or rosemary to purify and uplift the energies. A central altar is arranged, featuring symbols of balance and fertility: a chalice of water and a candle representing the union of feminine and masculine energies, fresh greens and blossoms for growth, and eggs or seeds to symbolize potential and rebirth.

The four directions may be acknowledged with corresponding elemental representations—earth with stones or soil in the north, air with a feather or incense in the east, fire with a candle or small flame in the south, and water in a bowl in the west. A circle is created using flowers, small stones, or natural markers, defining the sacred boundary within which the ceremony will unfold. As participants gather, moments of stillness or meditation help attune them to the energy of balance and renewal.

Before the ceremony begins, offerings of seeds, honey, or milk may be placed upon the altar as gifts to the earth and the spirits of the land. This reinforces the connection between the human and the natural world in celebration of turning the wheel toward longer, warmer days.

East-Air

Air embodies the mind, intellect, communication, new beginnings, and inspiration. The East, where the sun rises, symbolizes dawn, clarity, and the breath of life. The movement of air and wind is often associated with change and renewal. Its seasonal connection to spring reflects fresh growth and new ideas. The colors linked to the East are yellow, pale blue, and white. An invocation to the East may go something like this:

"O Spirit of the East, Breath of the Morning,
You who carry the whispers of the dawn,
We call upon you, Bringer of Inspiration,
Guardian of clarity, wisdom, and renewal.
From where the sun rises and the day begins,
Fill our minds with fresh ideas and clear intent.
Let your gentle winds sweep away the old,
And your mighty gales carry us toward change.
Bless this sacred space with your presence,
And guide us with your light and freedom.
Hail to the East, Element of Air!"

South-Fire

Fire signifies energy, passion, willpower, transformation, and creativity. The South corresponds to the sun at its peak, the warmth of midday, and the height of summer. It represents the vitality and intensity of life. This direction is tied to summer, a season of action, light, and warmth. Associated colors include red, orange, and gold.

"O Spirit of the South, Flame of Creation,
You who blaze with the light of midday,
We call upon you, Bearer of Passion,
Guardian of energy, courage, and transformation.
From where the sun reaches its zenith,
Ignite within us the fire of purpose and will.
Let your radiant warmth fill our hearts,
And your fierce flame burns away fear and doubt.
Bless this sacred space with your power,
And guide us with your strength and vitality.
Hail to the South, Element of Fire!"

West-Water

Water represents emotions, intuition, healing, reflection, and the subconscious. The West is connected to the setting sun, twilight, and bodies of water such as seas and rivers. It symbolizes the flow of life and the cycles of endings and beginnings. Its seasonal link to autumn marks a time when life slows down and turns inward. The colors associated with the West are blue, indigo, and sea green.

"O Spirit of the West, Keeper of the Depths,
You who dwell where the sun meets the sea,
We call upon you, Source of Intuition,
Guardian of emotions, healing, and reflection.
From where the waters flow, and dreams are born,
Cleanse our spirits with your gentle touch.

Let your currents carry us toward wisdom,
And your stillness teaches us peace.
Bless this sacred space with your presence,
And guide us with your depth and compassion.
Hail to the West, Element of Water!"

North-Earth

Earth signifies stability, grounding, abundance, fertility, and physicality. The North is often associated with mountains, cold winds, and the earth's solid, enduring foundation. It represents the unchanging and enduring aspects of nature. This direction corresponds to winter, a season of rest and conservation. The associated colors are earthy tones like green, brown, and black.

"O Spirit of the North, Pillar of Strength,
You who stand steadfast as the mountains,
We call upon you, Keeper of Stability,
Guardian of abundance, grounding, and wisdom.
From where the cold winds blow and the earth endures,
Anchor us in your unshakable presence.
Let your fertile soil nurture our growth,
And your ancient stones teach us resilience.
Bless this sacred space with your power,
And guide us with your steadfast protection.
Hail to the North, Element of Earth!"

Seeds are blessed and planted, symbolizing new beginnings and growth. This blessing honors the seeds as symbols of potential, growth, and the deep connection between the earth and the life cycle. It invokes the elements to nurture the seeds as they sprout, grow, and eventually bear fruit.

Druid blessing to honor and bless seeds:

"O Seeds of Life, tiny vessels of hope,
Held in the quiet of the earth's embrace,
We call upon the wisdom of the ancients,
To guide you in your sacred journey.
May the warmth of the sun nourish you,
May the rain of the heavens sustain you,
And may the winds of the earth carry you toward growth.
Blessed be your roots, that they may find strength in the soil,
Blessed be your leaves, that they may reach toward the sky,
And blessed be your fruit, that it may bring forth abundance.
As you grow, so too do we,
In harmony with the cycles of life and earth.
May your journey be one of balance, growth, and renewal,
And may your bounty be shared with all.
Hail to the seeds, the beginning of life's promise!"

An offering is made to the Earth, such as pouring water or scattering flower petals, in gratitude for nature's gifts. The following prayer ties together the elements of water and flower petals, symbolizing the earth's life force. It connects the offering to renewal, balance, and growth themes central to the Spring Equinox.

"Great Mother Earth, we come before you in reverence,
As the light returns and the days grow longer.
With humble hearts, we offer this gift of water and petals,
Symbols of the life that stirs within you and us.
May this water, drawn from the wellspring of your abundance,
Carry our gratitude and the blessings of renewal.
May it nourish the soil and cleanse the path ahead,
Opening the way for new growth, creativity, and wisdom.
May these petals, plucked from the flowers of the earth,
Represent the beauty and vitality of the season.
May they fall gently upon your sacred ground,
To honor the cycles of life, death, and rebirth.
As the balance of light and dark shifts,
So, do we seek harmony within ourselves?
Grant us strength to grow with the seasons,
And wisdom to understand the dance of creation.
Blessed Earth, we offer our love and respect,
And in return, we ask for your guidance, protection,
And the gifts of abundance that you so generously provide.
So be it; we honor the eternal cycle with hearts open to you."

Poem - The Song of the Spring

A traditional style of Druidic poetry often focused on nature, the elements, and seasonal changes. A short poem inspired by the themes of spring in Druidry might go something like this:

"Awake, O earth, from winter's sleep,

The flowers rise, and the willows weep.
From barren branches, buds unfold,
As sunlight breaks through skies of gold.
The winds of spring, they softly sing,
A melody of life's rebirth, they bring.
The rivers flow, the birds take wing,
And dance once more upon the earth.
O' seeds below, O skies above,
In springtime's warmth, we feel your love.
May all that's old now give way,
To greet the light of this new day."

This poem captures the essence of spring's awakening, celebrating the earth's rejuvenation and the return of life. It reflects the Druidic reverence for the cycles of nature, where each season plays a part in the ongoing dance of creation and transformation.

Chapter Three

Summer Solstice: Solar Power

The Summer Solstice, known in Druidry as Alban Hefin, or "The Light of the Shore," celebrates the longest day and the peak of the sun's power. It is a time of great energy, vitality, and joy when light reigns supreme, standing in perfect balance before beginning its slow retreat into the dark half of the year. The sun, the source of all life, is honored as it reaches its zenith, shining high and strong in the sky, bathing the earth in golden radiance. The Summer Solstice is a time for celebration and reflection, as Druids recognize the turning of the Wheel of the Year and the ever-present dance of light and shadow.

At Alban Hefin, the sun reaches the peak of its power, flooding the world with warmth and abundance. Yet, within this brilliance is an awareness of the impending decline. As the longest day passes, the days will gradually grow shorter, and the balance will tip again toward darkness. This festival conveys the wisdom of cycles—fullness and fading, rise and fall. Light cannot remain forever at its zenith, just as summer's bloom will yield to autumn's harvest. Druids embrace this understanding with reverence, recognizing that light and dark have their place in the grand cosmic rhythm.

Fire is central to the Summer Solstice rituals, mirroring the sun's power. Bonfires are lit on hilltops and sacred sites, with flames leaping skyward in homage to the solar force. These fires are believed to hold protective and purifying qualities, their flickering light warding off ill fortune and renewing the spirit. Leaping through the flames is an ancient tradition, symbolizing vitality, courage, and the forging of inner strength. As the fire burns, offerings are cast into the flames—herbs, flowers, and written prayers—offered as gifts to the divine to ask for blessings of health, prosperity, and protection in the months ahead.

The festival is also a time for floral offerings, as the land bursts with life. Flowers, especially sun-loving blooms such as marigolds, daisies, and roses, are gathered and woven into garlands or scattered upon the earth as gestures of gratitude. Sacred to the Druids, Oak is honored as the tree of midsummer, its strong and steadfast nature reflecting the sun's endurance. Some traditions also honor the Green Man, the spirit of the wild wood, whose face is seen in the leaves and whose energy courses through the vibrant world.

Dancing and singing are integral to the celebration of Alban Hefin, as Druids and revelers move in joyful rhythm beneath the midsummer sky. Spiral dances, sunwise processions, and lively music create a sense of unity with the natural world, echoing the pulse of life itself. Songs of praise for the sun, the earth, and the great turning of the year fill the air, lifting spirits and binding the community in shared reverence.

At the heart of the Summer Solstice lies the lesson of embracing the present moment—basking in life's fullness while recognizing the impermanence of all things. The sun's zenith reminds us to stand in our own power, celebrate our achievements, and prepare for the journey ahead as the wheel turns again.

Preparing the Ritual Space

Preparing a ritual space for the Druid ceremony of the Summer Solstice, or Alban Hefin, involves creating an environment that honors the height of the sun's power, the abundance of life, and the connection between earth and sky. Ideally, the ceremony takes place in an open, sunlit location such as a hilltop, a sacred stone circle, or near a body of water, where the expansive energy of the season can be fully embraced. If indoors, the space can be decorated with symbols of the sun's strength, including golden flowers like sunflowers and marigolds, bright-colored cloths, and candles to represent the peak of light.

Preparation begins with a ritual cleansing, such as wafting the space with purifying herbs like rosemary or sage, sprinkling water infused with midsummer blooms, or using bells and chanting to raise the vibrational energy. A central altar is set up to honor the sun, featuring a sun wheel or solar disk, a large candle or small fire, and offerings of summer fruits, grains, and mead to symbolize the earth's generosity. The four directions may be acknowledged with elemental representations—air in the east with feathers or incense, fire in the south with a flame or bright flowers, water in the west with a chalice or shell, and earth in the north with stones or freshly harvested herbs. A sacred circle is created using solar symbols, such as garlands of flowers, torches, or sun-marked stones, defining the ritual boundary.

As the ceremony begins, participants may meditate, absorbing the sun's warmth and energy, before engaging in dances, drumming, or offerings to celebrate the peak of light. The space is charged with joy and gratitude, as Alban Hefin marks not only the sun's zenith but also the turning point toward the darker half of the year, making it a time for both celebration and reflection.

Six Druid Invocations for the Summer Solstice (Alban Hefin)

Invocation to the Sun at Its Zenith

"O Radiant One, Golden King of the sky,
At your peak, you bless the land with light and life.
Your fire kindles the heart of the world,
Your warmth awakens the fields and forests.
We honor you, great Sun, in your full strength,
And offer our gratitude for your endless gift.
Shine upon us, within us, around us
Until the wheel turns again."

Invocation of Fire and Flame

"Sacred fire, burning bright,
Mirror of the mighty Sun,
Your flickering tongues reach to the heavens,
Carrying our prayers on golden wings.
Cleanse us, strengthen us, guide us forth,
As we stand in the heart of summer's light.
By flame and ember, we honor the fire within."

Invocation to the Oak and the Green Man

"O mighty Oak, guardian of Midsummer's crown,

Your roots hold the wisdom of ages past,
Your branches reach to the light of tomorrow.
Green Man, spirit of the wild wood,
Your laughter dances in the whispering leaves,
Your breath fills the summer air with life.
Bless us with your strength, your wisdom, your wild joy
That we may walk in harmony with all that grows."

Blessing of the Flowers

"Blossoms of gold, petals of fire,
Born of the sun's warm embrace,
We gather you in joy and love,
To weave the beauty of this day into our hearts.
By rose and daisy, by oak and fern,
May the blessings of midsummer surround us.
Earth, sea, and sky, receive our thanks."

Song of the Turning Wheel

"Light and shadow, night and day,
The wheel turns, yet we stand still,
In the fullness of this golden hour.
The sun has risen to its throne,
And soon shall take the path of descent.
We honor this moment, bright and fleeting,
And dance within the balance of all things.
Blessed be the rhythm of the land."

Farewell to the Longest Day

"O great Sun, your journey begins anew,
Though your fire still burns bright within us.
As your golden chariot turns toward the west,
We carry your light in our hearts and souls.
Guide us through the days that darken,
Let your memory kindle our spirit and strength.
We bid farewell to the longest day
Until we meet again at the turning of the wheel."

Chapter Four

Autumn Equinox: The Slowing of Nature

The Autumn Equinox, known in Druidry as Alban Elfed, or "The Light of the Water," is a time of balance, gratitude, and transition. On this sacred day, light and darkness are equal, marking when the sun's strength wanes and the descent into the darker half of the year begins. It is a time to honor both the abundance of the harvest and the wisdom of letting go, as the earth prepares to rest.

Alban Elfed is deeply connected to the final gathering of crops, the culmination of the efforts made during the bright half of the year. Druids recognize this festival as a time of thanksgiving, offering gratitude to the land, the elements, and the spirits that have helped bring sustenance and prosperity. Fruits, grains, and vegetables are often shared in feasts and offerings, symbolizing the gifts of the earth and the importance of reciprocity with nature. The equinox reminds us that all things move in cycles—what is gathered now will sustain us through the coming cold, just as the lessons learned in this season will guide us in the months ahead.

At this time of balance, Druids also reflect on their lives, seeking harmony between work and rest, giving and receiving, light and shadow. It is a moment to recognize both achievement and the necessity of surrender—just as the trees begin to shed their leaves, we too must release what no longer serves us.

Rituals for Alban Elfed may include offerings of apples and grains, ceremonies by water to honor the flow of time, and quiet meditation on the changing seasons. It is a time of celebration and preparation, a reminder that as the nights lengthen, the wisdom of the dark is just as sacred as the brilliance of the light.

Preparation of the Ritual Space

Preparing a ritual space for the Druid ceremony of the Autumn Equinox, or Alban Elfed, involves creating an environment that reflects the balance between light and dark, as well as gratitude for the harvest and preparation for the coming winter. Ideally, the ritual takes place in a natural setting, such as a forest clearing, an orchard, or beside a river or lake, where the shifting colors of the season and the crispness of the air can be fully experienced. If held indoors, the space is decorated with harvest symbols—sheaves of grain, apples, pumpkins, acorns, and richly colored leaves—to honor the earth's abundance.

The preparation begins with cleansing the space, using incense such as frankincense or myrrh, a sprinkling of blessed water, or the sounding of bells or chimes to clear and balance the energy. A central altar is arranged with offerings of seasonal fruits, bread, and wine or cider, representing the gifts of the land and the gratitude of the participants. The four directions are acknowledged with elemental symbols: a feather or incense in the east for air, a candle or autumn flowers in the south for fire, a bowl of water in the west, and a stone, acorns, or grains in the north for earth. A sacred circle is created using leaves, harvested produce, or lanterns, marking the ritual space where participants will gather.

As the ceremony begins, moments of reflection or meditation help align the participants with the season's themes of balance, release, and gratitude. The space is infused with a sense of completion and transition, recognizing that while the light wanes, the wisdom and nourishment of the harvest will sustain both body and spirit through the darker months ahead.

The imagined prayer below reflects the Druidic understanding of the autumn equinox as a time of balance, where light and dark are acknowledged as necessary for the cycles of life. It embraces the transition into the darker months, honoring rest, renewal, and the wisdom found in stillness.

"O Great Spirit of the Earth,
In this sacred time of balance,
We honor the turning of the wheel,
The light wanes, and darkness draws near.
O Cailleach, Keeper of Winter's Veil,
We thank you for the quieting of the land,
For the rest you bring to the earth,
As you prepare us for the renewal to come.
O Cernunnos, Horned One, Lord of the Wild,
We honor your presence in the changing seasons,
In the harvest of abundance, and the promise of rest
Your horns carry the wisdom of life and death intertwined.
As day and night find their balance,
We acknowledge the darkness with gratitude,

For it is in the quiet shadows that we find rest,
And in stillness, we are restored.
We honor the need for darkness to guide us,
To prepare the soil for new growth and fertile seeds,
And to allow time for reflection and renewal
So we may rise again with the light.
In this moment of perfect balance,
We release the old, that which no longer serves,
And welcome the stillness, the peace, and the mystery,
Trusting that all things are part of the sacred dance.
May the dark nurture us, as the light has nourished,
And may we honor both with open hearts,
As we stand in the balance of the seasons,
And trust in the eternal cycle of life and rebirth.
So be it."

The invocations below honor specific parts of ritual and can be spoken in ritual, during feasts, or as personal prayers at Alban Elfed. They embrace the themes of gratitude, balance, and transition.

Invocation of Balance

"O Great Wheel, turn in perfect grace,
Light and dark now stand embraced.
Day and night in equal measure,
Moment held in sacred tether.
Teach us balance, wise and true,
As we walk this path anew."

Blessing of the Harvest

"Blessed be the gifts of the land,
Fruit and grain by nature's hand.
Through sun and rain, through wind and toil,
The earth has yielded golden spoil.
With grateful hearts, we now receive,
And vow to honor, not deceive.
May we share, may we give,
May all be fed, may all souls live."

Invocation of Letting Go

"As leaves release from branch to ground,
So too must we set burdens down.
What is ripe, we now shall reap,
What has served, we lay to sleep.
Guide our hands, O autumn's breath,
To part with grace, to dance with death.
In falling, rising is begun
The wheel turns, the two are one."

Calling to the Spirits of the Land

"O spirits of field, forest, and stream,
Guardians of fruit, of root, of dream,
We honor you in this time of change,
As the earth prepares for rest again.
Bless these gifts, this sacred ground,
May peace and wisdom here be found."

Prayer to the Waters of Life

"O waters deep, O rivers wide,
Flowing strong with ancient tide.
Mirror of the twilight's hue,
Keeper of the old and new.
May your currents cleanse and guide,
As we stand where dark and light collide.
Bless the seasons, bless this space,
May we move with nature's grace."

Farewell to the Sun's Strength

"Golden Sun, your fire fades low,
Your journey shifts, your pace now slows.
We honor all you've given bright,
The days of warmth, the skies of light.
Now rest, O Sun, in winter's keep,
Until you wake from longest sleep.
We hold your ember deep inside
And wait for when you rise in pride."

Chapter Five

Imbolc Ritual: A Time of Cleansing and Purification

Imbolc, celebrated on February 1st or 2nd, marked the midpoint between winter and spring. It was a festival of light, renewal, and fertility, dedicated to the goddess Brigid, who was associated with poetry, healing, smithcraft, and the hearth. The festival heralded the first signs of spring, such as the lambing season, and celebrated the return of longer days and the rekindling of life.

While specific Druidic Imbolc rituals are not recorded, reconstructions rely on historical texts, archaeological evidence, and surviving Celtic traditions.

The Imbolc ritual honored the return of light and life after winter, invoked blessings for crops, livestock, and the community, and purified the home and hearth, making space for new beginnings.

The ritual was often performed near sacred wells, springs, or hearths, as these were associated with Brigid. A communal fire in the village or a sacred grove (*nemeton*) could also be the focal point.

Components of the Ritual

Druids, or in some cases a priestess devoted to Brigid, led the rituals. They invoked Brigid's blessings, facilitated offerings, and guided participants through the ceremonial acts. Community members, including families, farmers, and craftspeople, participated actively.

The ritual area was cleansed with fire, water, or smoke from burning herbs like sage or juniper. An altar was adorned with Brigid symbols, such as candles, woven rush crosses (Brigid's crosses), and offerings of milk, bread, and seeds.

Leaders wore ceremonial robes, often white or green, symbolizing purity, renewal, and the promise of spring. They might carry staffs or wands and wear greenery garlands. People dressed in clean, simple garments, often incorporating symbols of spring, like floral decorations or green and gold hues. Some women wore veils or headscarves in honor of Brigid.

The Druids called upon Brigid, invoking her aspects as a goddess of fire, fertility, and creativity. This might involve chants, poems, or songs in her honor.

A sacred fire was kindled, symbolizing the warmth and light of the returning sun. All participants gathered around the fire, which served as the ritual's focal point.

Preparing the Ritual Space

Preparing a ritual space for the Druid ceremony of Imbolc involves creating an environment that reflects the themes of purification, renewal, and the first stirrings of life after winter's darkness. Ideally, the ritual is held in a natural setting, such as near a flowing stream, within a grove of trees, or in a quiet meadow where the earliest signs of spring—snowdrops, lambs, and lengthening days—can be observed. If performed indoors, the space can be adorned with white candles, fresh flowers, and symbols of Brigid, the goddess of fertility, poetry, and healing, whose presence is honored during this festival.

The preparation begins with cleansing the area using sacred water, smudging with purifying herbs such as rosemary or juniper, or gently ringing bells to clear away stagnant winter energies. A central altar is set up, featuring white and green candles to represent purity and growth, a bowl of water for cleansing and blessing, and a small dish of seeds to symbolize the potential of new life. The four directions are acknowledged with elemental offerings: incense or feathers in the east for air, a candle or small flame in the south for fire, a bowl of water or a seashell in the west, and stones, soil, or early spring flowers in the north for earth. A sacred circle may be outlined with candles, woven straw, or small white stones, defining the ritual space.

Before the ceremony begins, participants may engage in silent reflection or meditation, focusing on personal renewal and setting intentions for the year ahead. The space is imbued with a sense of quiet anticipation and reverence, as Imbolc marks the transition from winter's stillness to the gradual awakening of the earth, making it a time for both introspection and celebration of the light's return.

Chant for the Awakening of the Earth

Imbolc celebrates the first stirrings of life beneath the still-winter earth. A chant dedicated to the earth's awakening helps set the tone for the festival.

"Awaken, earth, with gentle grace,
Bring forth the light, a new dawn's face.
From deep below, the green will rise,
And meet the warmth of spring's blue skies."

This chant honors the earth as it begins to awaken from its winter slumber and prepares to receive the first signs of spring.

Offerings

To Brigid: Offerings of milk (symbolizing livestock fertility), grains, butter, and other foods were presented at the altar or poured into sacred wells and springs. Crafted items, such as woven Brigid's crosses made of rushes or straw, were placed on the altar or in homes for protection and blessings.

To the Earth: Seeds were blessed and ceremonially scattered, symbolizing the hope for a bountiful harvest.

Offering Chants

Imbolc rituals may also include offerings to Brigid, such as milk, bread, and candles. These offerings are often accompanied by chants that express gratitude and honor.

"We offer milk, we offer bread,
Brigid, bless us, as we've said.
By your fire, by your flame,

We call on you to bless our name."

This chant is used when presenting offerings, invoking Brigid's blessings for fertility, prosperity, and protection in the coming year.

The Blessing of the Waters

Water is a key element in Imbolc rituals, often symbolizing purification and renewal. Chanting over water can be part of the ceremony to bless and invoke the goddess's powers.

"Water of life, so clear and pure,
Brigid's blessing will endure.
From the well, from the stream,
Bring to us your sacred dream."

This chant can bless water used in rituals or offerings, invoking Brigid's healing and nurturing powers.

Blessing the Hearth and Home

A piece of cloth or a small garment, Brigid's Mantle, was placed outside overnight to absorb her blessings. This cloth was brought in during the ritual to bless the home, livestock, and people.

Participants extinguished their hearth fires at home and relit them using flames from the sacred fire, symbolizing renewal and unity with the divine.

Purification Chants

Imbolc is a time of cleansing and purification, so rituals often include chants focused on clearing away the old to make room for the new.

"By the light of the sacred flame,
I purify and call your name.
Brigid's fire, burning bright,
Cleanse this space and bless this night."

This chant invokes Brigid's purifying fire to cleanse the space and the participants, symbolizing the removal of winter's stagnant energy.

Fertility and Cleansing Rituals

Farmers brought livestock, especially sheep (associated with Brigid), to the ritual site for blessings. The Druids passed a flame or smoke over the animals to ensure their health and fertility.

Participants walked through or around the fire or were anointed with water from a sacred well to cleanse themselves of lingering negativity and prepare for the new season.

The Circle of Fire

Imbolc rituals frequently include fire as a central element, honoring the goddess Brigid's association with fire and light. Participants might chant or sing around a flame to invoke her energy.

"Fire, fire, shining bright,
Guide us through this winter's night.
Brigid's flame, we call on thee,
Light the way for all to see."

Invocation to Brigid

Brigid is the central figure of Imbolc, and the rituals include invocations to her. These invocations honor her as the goddess of fire, fertility, and inspiration.

"Brigid, Brigid, flame of light,
Guide us through the long winter night.
Goddess of fire, of hearth and home,
Bless us as we journey to the spring's warm throne.
Brigid, bright and shining one,
Bring the warmth of the returning sun.
With your fire, the earth renew,
We honor you, Brigid, ever true."

This invocation calls on Brigid to bless the participants with warmth, light, and renewal.

The Creation of the Brigid's Cross

A significant tradition during Imbolc is the crafting of Brigid's Cross, a symbol of protection and a way to honor the goddess. This cross, a smaller variant of the Christian cross, is traditionally woven from straw or rushes. It comes in various shapes; the earliest forms were simple Christian Latin or Greek crosses, but the most common modern version features a woven diamond or lozenge at its center. The cross is named after the Christian saint Brigid of Kildare.

Brigid's Cross is typically woven from straw or rushes on February 1st, her feast day, as well as during the Imbolc festival in pre-Christian Ireland. It was believed that hanging the cross from the rafters of one's home would invite the blessing and protection of the saint throughout the year.

As part of the ritual, a chant may accompany the weaving of the cross.

"We weave the cross, the sacred sign,
Brigid's blessing to intertwine.
With each twist and with each turn,
We honor her, we honor her."

This chant helps focus participants on the sacredness of the cross they are weaving, invoking Brigid's blessings for the home.

Closing the Ritual

The Druids invoked Brigid one last time, thanking her for her presence and blessings. Participants took home embers from the fire or water from the sacred well to spread her blessings throughout their homes and fields.

The ritual concluded with a communal meal featuring dairy products, bread, and other foods associated with the season. This reinforced communal ties and celebrated the abundance to come.

Closing Invocation

To close an Imbolc ritual, participants often offer a final invocation of thanks and farewell to Brigid and the other deities, asking for continued guidance and protection.

"Brigid, goddess, bright and true,
We thank you for the light you grew.
As we leave, your flame we take,
In our hearts, your fire will wake."

Chapter Six

Beltane Ritual: A Celebration of Spring and Fertility

Beltane, or Alban Bealtaine, is the festival of fire and fertility, marking the height of spring and the transition into summer. Celebrated on May 1st, it is a time of passion, vitality, and union between the seen and unseen worlds. Beltane is the counterpart to Samhain, with both festivals existing at the threshold between seasons, when the veil between worlds is at its thinnest. While Samhain honors death and the ancestors, Beltane celebrates life, love, and renewal. It is a time when Druids and celebrants welcome the growing power of the sun, call upon the spirits of the land, and honor the sacred union between masculine and feminine energies in nature.

Central to Beltane is the fire ritual, reflecting the sun's strength as it rises toward its midsummer peak. Huge bonfires were lit upon hills and sacred sites, and people would dance around them, leaping through the flames for purification, protection, and blessing. Cattle and livestock were driven between fires to ensure fertility and good health for the coming year. The Maypole dance, another key tradition, represented the weaving of life's forces, as brightly colored ribbons spiraled around the pole in a sacred, joyful movement.

Beltane was also a time for handfasting rituals, symbolic weddings that temporarily bound couples together for a year and a day or life. Milk, honey, and flowers were offered to nature spirits, the Fae, and the gods, seeking their favor and protection. Many retreated into the wild for meditation and vision quests, seeking guidance from the land and the ancestors.

At its heart, Beltane is a festival of ecstasy, creation, and the wild spirit of nature, calling all who celebrate to embrace life's fire with joy and reverence.

Preparation of the Ritual Space

Preparing a ritual space for the Druid ceremony of Beltane involves creating an environment that celebrates fertility, passion, and the vibrant energy of life's renewal. Ideally, the ritual takes place outdoors in a lush meadow, a flowering grove, or near a sacred fire, where nature's abundance and the season's warmth can be fully embraced. If held indoors, the space is decorated with bright ribbons, fresh flowers, and symbols of fire and fertility, such as red and white candles, woven garlands, and bowls of fruit and honey.

The preparation begins with cleansing the area, using fragrant herbs like hawthorn, lavender, or rosemary, either scattered on the ground or burned as incense to purify and bless the space. A central altar is arranged, featuring symbols of Beltane's union of masculine and feminine energies—perhaps a chalice of water and a candle, a floral wreath, or figurines representing the god and goddess. A small cauldron or fire pit is often placed at the heart of the space to represent the sacred Beltane fire, which is traditionally kindled to mark the transition into the light half of the year. The four directions are honored with corresponding elemental offerings: incense or a feather in the east for air, a candle or flame in the south for fire, a bowl of water or fresh flowers in the west, and stones or fertile soil in the north for earth. A sacred circle may be outlined with flowers, ribbons, or lanterns, defining the boundary of the ritual space.

Before the ceremony begins, participants may walk or dance around the space to raise energy, weave ribbons around a Maypole, or jump over small fires or candles as a symbolic act of purification and blessing. The ritual space is charged with joy, sensuality, and celebration, as Beltane marks the height of spring's vitality, the sacred union of divine forces, and the call to fully embrace life's creative energies.

Preparatory charm

"Great gods and goddesses of life and creation,
We give thanks for your blessings of fertility and abundance.
May this fire burn brightly as a beacon of hope,
And may its flames carry our prayers to the heavens.
As spring ripens into summer,
May our hearts be full and our spirits renewed.
We walk this path in honor of you. So may it be."

A Delightful Alternative

"Spirits of the land, the rivers, and the skies,
Ancient ones who dwell unseen,
We honor your presence this sacred night.
Guardians of forest and field,
Guide our steps with wisdom and care.
May your energies bless this circle,
And may our offerings find favor with you.
With respect and love, we give thanks. So may it be."

The Maypole is deeply symbolic, representing fertility and the renewal of life. Its upright form, combined with weaving and decorating, reflects the union of masculine and feminine energies in nature. As a key element of May Day festivities, it celebrates spring's arrival, crops' growth, and the promise of abundance. The communal dance around the maypole also embodies harmony, cooperation, and strengthening community bonds.

"O Earth Mother, giver of life,
We honor your fertile soil and sacred lands.
Bless our fields, our homes, and our hearts,
That we may thrive in harmony with your bounty.
As the wheel turns, may your abundance grow,
And may we walk gently upon your sacred ground.
In gratitude, we offer this prayer. So may it be."

Opening the Ritual

The Druids invoked deities or spirits associated with fertility, fire, and the land. Some deities linked to these are Brighid (Brigid), and Belisama, a goddess of light and fire, the forge, and crafts. She is associated with healing springs and is the wife of the god Belinus. Cernunnos is recognized as the god of fertility, abundance, regeneration, and wild animals. Often depicted with antlers, he embodies the vitality of nature and the land. Lastly, Belenus (Belinus) is a god associated with light called "The Shining One." He oversees the welfare of sheep and cattle and is linked to the land's prosperity.

"Great Belisama, guardian of light and fire,
We honor your presence and seek your blessing.
Ignite within us the flame of inspiration,
Nurture our endeavors with your fertile essence,
ground us in the sacredness of the earth.
May your guidance lead us to harmony and abundance. So be it."

The sacred Beltane fire was lit, symbolizing the sun's power and the purifying force of light. All other fires in the community were extinguished beforehand, and new flames were kindled from the Beltane fire.

"Bright Sun, golden flame of life,
You rise and light the path before us.
Bless our crops, our livestock, and our days,
With your warmth, bring growth and renewal.
Guide us with your light as the seasons turn,
And keep us ever in balance with the wheel of time.
We thank you for your blessings. So may it be."

Closing the Ritual

The Druids thanked the deities and spirits, offering final prayers for protection and prosperity. A closing prayer might go something like this:

"Deities of light, spirits of the wild,
We close this sacred circle with reverence.
May the bonds we've forged in this fire's glow
Remain strong as we step into the growing season.
Guide our steps, bless our hearts,
And keep us united as one community.
In your name, we honor the cycles of life. So may it be."

Chapter Seven

Lughnasadh Ritual: Honoring the Harvest

Lughnasadh, also referred to as Alban Elfed or the Feast of Lugh, is the first harvest festival, celebrated around August 1st. It signifies the beginning of the reaping season, when the grains sown in spring have matured and the earth's bounty is collected. In Druid tradition, Lughnasadh is a time of gratitude, sacrifice, and community, as the balance between light and dark shifts toward the autumn equinox. It is a festival of both celebration and solemnity, honoring the labor that has yielded abundance while acknowledging the sacrifices that ensure the cycle of life persists.

At the heart of Lughnasadh ceremonies is the figure of Lugh, the multi-talented god of light, crafts, and sovereignty. Though named for Lugh, the festival is thought to have been established by him in tribute to his foster mother, Tailtiu, an earth goddess who passed away from exhaustion after clearing the land for agriculture. Thus, Lughnasadh is a time of harvest and feasting and a recognition of the sacrifices made for prosperity, whether by the gods, the land, or the people who work it.

Druidic rituals during Lughnasadh often feature the blessing of the first fruits, particularly grains, which were once transformed into sacred loaves of bread and offered to the gods and spirits of the land. Feasting is central to the celebration, with ceremonial sharing of bread, fruit, and ale, acknowledging the gifts of the earth and the significance of community. Fire ceremonies are also prevalent, symbolizing the power of the sun, which has nurtured the crops but is now beginning its decline as the year shifts toward autumn.

Another essential aspect of Lughnasadh is the games and contests, which reflect Lugh's warrior and champion traits. Athletic competitions, storytelling, and exhibitions of skill were part of the ancient festival, promoting strength, resilience, and camaraderie. Some Druidic groups also include handfasting rituals, as this was traditionally a time for unions and betrothals, ensuring the continuity of life and prosperity.

As a transition festival, Lughnasadh reminds Druids of the ever-turning Wheel of the Year. It is a time to reflect on personal growth, reap the rewards of efforts made, and prepare for the upcoming months of gathering and storage. While it is a joyful celebration of life's abundance, it also conveys the wisdom of impermanence—just as the harvest must be collected, the warmth of summer will soon yield to the darker days of the year.

In the Lughnasadh ritual, Lugh is invoked to bless the harvest, ensuring its abundance and fertility, as well as the prosperity of the people. The rituals often involved offerings of grains, bread, fruits, and mead, celebrating Lugh's role in bringing forth the earth's bounty. Symbolically, the offerings represent gratitude for the harvest and the hope for continued fertility in the coming seasons. Lugh's association with light and the sun also means that his festival marks a time of transition—celebrating the fullness of summer while acknowledging the slow approach of autumn and the darker months.

Preparing the Ritual Space

Preparing a ritual space for the Druid ceremony of Lughnasadh, involves creating an environment that honors the first harvest, the turning of the seasons, and the interplay of effort and abundance. Ideally, the ritual is held outdoors in a golden field, an orchard, or atop a hill, where summer's ripening grains and fruits can be seen and appreciated. If held indoors, the space is decorated with sheaves of wheat, corn, sunflowers, and baskets of bread, apples, and berries to symbolize the gifts of the earth.

The preparation begins with a ritual cleansing, such as burning herbs like sage or mugwort, sprinkling blessed water around the space, or using the rhythmic beating of a drum to awaken the land's energy. A central altar is arranged, displaying symbols of the harvest—a loaf of freshly baked bread, grains, seasonal fruits, and a sickle or scythe to represent the cycle of reaping and sowing. The four directions are honored with elemental offerings: incense or a feather in the east for air, a candle or dried chili peppers in the south for fire, a bowl of water or a cup of mead in the west, and a bundle of wheat, corn, or soil in the north for earth. A sacred circle may be marked with harvested grains, stones, or small torches, defining the boundary for the ritual.

Before the ceremony begins, moments of gratitude and reflection are encouraged, allowing participants to acknowledge the fruits of their labor and the sacrifices required for abundance. The space is infused with a sense of thanksgiving and transition, as Lughnasadh marks the height of summer's bounty and the first signs of the waning year, reminding everyone of the ongoing growth, harvest, and renewal cycles.

The Druids or ritual leaders would then invoke the divine energy of Lugh, the god of craftsmanship and the harvest, asking for his blessing and favor on the tools. They might also call on other gods and spirits associated with the earth, fertility, and nature to provide protection, fertility, and success in the upcoming season. The tools would be sprinkled with sacred water or oil or touched by the Druid's staff or blade to consecrate them.

Invocation of Lugh

"O Lugh, shining god of the harvest,
we call upon your skill and mastery.
Bless these tools, gifts of earth and craft,
that they may work with strength and purpose.
Grant them the power to cultivate the land
and create in harmony with the cycles of the seasons.
May our labor be fruitful and our craft precise.
In your name, we honor these tools,
and through them, may we honor the land, the sky, and the people. So be it."

Invocation to Lugh

"Hail to Lugh, Master of the Light,
Shining bright as the summer's height.
God of craft and endless skill,
We honor you with hearts that will,
Bring forth the bounty from the land,
Blessed by your divine hand.

Lugh of the Sun, of fire and flame,
We call upon your sacred name.
Grant us your wisdom, your guiding light,
Through the darkening hours of night.
Bless this harvest, bless our home,
That we may never feel alone.
We offer our thanks, both high and low,
For the gifts of the earth, as you bestow.
Bless this day, and all who gather near,
With your strength, your vision, and your cheer.
Hail Lugh, of shining sun and moon,
Guide us through the harvest's boon."

Blessing of the Farming Tools

"Great Earth, Great Sky, we offer these tools of the harvest,
that they may be blessed in your name.
With this sickle, may we cut what is ripe
and bring abundance to our homes.
With this plow, may the soil yield its bounty.
We ask for your protection over these implements,
that they may work as extensions of our will,
guided by the wisdom of the land.
May they be strong, resilient, and fruitful,
bringing us the earth's gifts and the sun's blessings. So may it be."

Blessing of Artisanal Tools

"O Lugh, god of creation and craft,
bless these tools we use to shape and form the world.

With this hammer, may we strike with precision and strength.
With this chisel, may we carve with clarity and beauty.
May our hands work in harmony with the spirit of the materials,
and may we create works that honor the earth, the gods, and the people.
May our craft be blessed, our intentions clear,
and our skill ever growing. In your name, we offer these tools. So be it."

Blessing with Sacred Water or Oil

"By the waters of the sacred well, we bless these tools.
As the water cleanses the earth,
so may this blessing cleanse and empower these implements.
Let them work in harmony with the forces of nature,
bringing forth the fruits of the earth and the fruits of the craft.
May they never falter in their purpose
and may the blessings of the gods be ever upon them.
May Lugh guide their use
and fill our hearts with the wisdom to work with honor and joy. So it is."

General Blessing for Tools

"By the strength of the sun and the fertility of the earth,
we bless these tools.
Let them carry our work, our intentions,
and our desires into the world.
May they cut, carve, mold, and shape with the grace of the divine,
bringing abundance, creativity, and skill into all that we do.
We ask for protection and prosperity in the season ahead,
that our efforts may be met with bounty and our hearts with joy.
May this blessing extend to all who use these tools,

in the name of Lugh and all the gods. So be it."

Closing the Ritual

In the closing ritual of the Lughnasadh ceremony, prayers and invocations are a way to honor Lugh, the god of harvest, craftsmanship, and the sun, as well as other deities tied to abundance, prosperity, and protection. These prayers serve as expressions of gratitude for the gifts of the season, for the land's fertility, and to ask for blessings for the upcoming months. Here are a few prayers that may be used:

Prayer to Lugh

"Great Lugh, shining lord of the harvest,
With your golden hand, you bless the fields,
From your light, the crops ripen and grow,
From your wisdom, we reap what we sow.
We thank you for the bounty of the land,
For the grain, the fruit, the work of our hands.
May your brilliance continue to guide us,
As the sun's power wanes and the earth turns.
Grant us skill in our craft and strength in our work,
Let us walk in harmony with the cycles of life,
Bless us with abundance in the coming year,
And protect us in the dark months to come.
Lugh, we honor you, we praise your name,
In your light, we stand, and in your harvest, we claim."

Prayer for the Earth and the Harvest

"Blessed Earth, mother of abundance,
From your womb, we gather the gifts of the season.

We honor the soil, the rain, and the sun,
The forces that nourish and make us one.
May the grain grow tall and the fruit ripen sweet,
May the harvest be plentiful and all needs be met.
We give thanks for what you provide,
And ask that your bounty may never subside.
May the winds of the coming season bring us peace,
And may we share with others the wealth we receive.
We honor you, Earth, in this time of abundance,
May your blessings flow with each passing season."

Prayer to the Ancestors and Spirits of the Land

"Spirits of the land, guardians of the soil,
We thank you for your patience and toil.
Ancestors who watched and tended before,
We offer our thanks and open the door.
May your wisdom guide us in every step,
In every seed we plant, in every harvest kept.
We honor you, we remember your name,
And from your gifts, we do not claim fame.
May we live in harmony, as you once did,
With reverence for nature and all that it gives.
Spirits, we honor you, in gratitude and grace,
Guide our hands and hearts as we walk in this place."

Prayer for Protection and Prosperity

"Great guardians, protectors of our home,
Bless this community, where we've chosen to roam.

May your spirits keep us safe from harm,
May the light of your wisdom bring peace and calm.
Bless our work, our families, and all that we share,
Let prosperity grow in abundance, without despair.
May the coming seasons bring us grace,
And may the fruits of our labor fill every space.
We ask for protection from the shadows of night,
And the strength to endure until the next light.
As we close this circle, we walk with you,
With courage and hope, our hearts remain true."

Prayer of Gratitude and Farewell

"To Lugh, to the Earth, and the Spirits of the Land,
We offer thanks with open hearts and hands.
The harvest is plentiful, the sun still bright,
But soon, the days will shorten with the coming of night.
May we walk through the darkness with the light of your grace,
And return in the spring to once again embrace.
Until that time, we bid you farewell,
But in our hearts, your love will dwell.
Blessings to the land, to the seeds we sow,
May we return to you when it's time to grow?
Farewell for now, but not for long,
In your light and wisdom, we'll remain strong."

These prayers offer gratitude for the current harvest, request blessings for the future, and honor the gods, spirits, and ancestors who have supported the community throughout the year. They are spoken aloud by the ritual leader or chanted by the community, strengthening the connection to the divine and the land.

Chapter Eight

Samhain Ritual: Ancient Halloween

Samhain, celebrated around October 31st to November 1st, marked the end of the Celtic year and the transition into winter. Liminality implies an element of transition or change. Within liminal festivals, there is a celebration of the past and a look to the future. As a liminal festival, it was a time when the veil between the worlds of the living and the dead was believed to be the thinnest. As spiritual leaders, Druids played a central role in Samhain rituals, orchestrating ceremonies to honor the dead, ensure the community's safety, and secure blessings for the coming year. This was a "supernaturally charged" time of year when the dead could make their escape.

While no direct records exist of specific Druidic Samhain rituals, modern reconstructions draw from archaeological findings, ancient texts, and comparative anthropology.

At Samhain (which corresponds to modern Halloween), time lost all meaning, and the past, present, and future were one. The dead and the denizens of the Other World walked among the living. It was a time of fairies, ghosts, demons, and witches. Winter was the Season of Ghosts, and Samhain was the night of their release from the Underworld. Many people lit bonfires to keep the evil spirits at bay. Often, a torch was lit and carried around the boundaries of the home and farm to protect the property and residents against the spirits throughout the winter.

The ritual honors the ancestors and spirits of the dead and communicates with the Otherworld for guidance or blessings. The ancient Druid practice was to circle the tribal Samhain bonfire with the skulls of their ancestors, who would protect the tribe from demons that night. Samhain marks the end of the harvest and prepares for the hardships of winter. It strengthens bonds within the tribe and invokes protection from malevolent forces.

The ritual is typically performed outdoors in a sacred grove (*nemeton*) or near a hilltop where the sky and natural elements are visible. A central bonfire acted as the ritual's focal point, symbolizing purification, transformation, and unity.

Druids conducted the ceremonies while the tribe gathered to observe and partake. Each family extinguished their hearth fires, symbolizing the end of the old year, to be relit from the communal bonfire. A stone or wooden altar was set up with offerings such as harvested grains, fruits, milk, and meat. Ritual tools included ceremonial knives or sickles (possibly bronze or iron), wands, and cauldrons for offerings or divination. Talismans, such as carved stones, animal bones, or symbolic charms, were used for protection and blessings.

Participants likely wore white robes symbolizing purity or adorned themselves with ceremonial cloaks of animal skins, particularly wolf or stag, symbolizing their connection to nature and the spiritual realm. Some Druids may have worn oak-leaf crowns to emphasize their sacred connection to trees and divine wisdom. Members of the tribe donned simple woolen or linen clothing. Masks or disguises were often worn to confuse wandering spirits, reflecting the belief in veil thinning. The mask is a sacred necessity to these ritual festivals and is intertwined with the fundamental notions of Samhain as a festival of death and the transition into winter.

Participants gathered in a circle around the bonfire. Druids invoked deities or spirits of the land, calling for their presence and blessings. The sacred bonfire was lit using a ceremonial flame, possibly kindled by striking flint or through a sun wheel to symbolize the continuity of life and the sun's return after winter.

Offerings were placed on the altar or cast into the fire to honor the dead and seek their guidance. This could include food, drink, and symbolic items. Personal tokens, such as family heirlooms or small carvings, might be presented to connect with specific ancestors. Druids offered prayers and chants to appease spirits and ensure they would not harm the community.

Preparing the Ritual Space

Preparing a ritual space for the Druid ceremony of Samhain involves creating an environment that honors the thinning of the veil between worlds, the ancestors, and the transition into the dark half of the year. Ideally, the ritual takes place outdoors in a quiet forest clearing, near an ancient tree, or beside a fire, where the natural world reflects the deep stillness of the season. If held indoors, the space is decorated with autumn leaves, gourds, dried herbs, and candles to create an atmosphere of reverence and introspection.

The preparation begins with a ritual cleansing, using smoke from mugwort or rosemary to purify the space, sprinkling blessed water for protection, or softly ringing bells to clear stagnant energy. A central altar is arranged with symbols of Samhain—black and orange candles for death and rebirth, photographs or mementos of ancestors, offerings of seasonal fruits, nuts, and mead, and a skull or cauldron to represent the mysteries of transformation. The four directions are honored with elemental offerings: incense or a feather in the east for air, a candle or lantern in the south for fire, a bowl of water or autumn flowers in the west, and a stone or dried leaves in the north for earth. A sacred circle may be marked with candles, bones, or fallen branches, defining the boundary between the mundane and the sacred.

Before the ceremony begins, moments of silent reflection or guided meditation help participants attune to the energies of the season and connect with the spirits of their ancestors. The space is imbued with a deep sense of mystery and reverence, as Samhain marks the end of the old year and the beginning of a new cycle, a time for honoring the past, embracing transformation, and seeking wisdom from the unseen realms.

Invocations for a Samhain Ritual

Samhain, or Alban Hefin, is the festival of endings and beginnings, when the veil between the worlds is at its thinnest. It is a night for honoring the ancestors, embracing transformation, seeking wisdom, and preparing for winter's dark embrace. The following invocations can be used throughout a Samhain ritual, encompassing all aspects of the celebration.

Opening Invocation: The Veil Grows Thin

"On this night of shadows deep,

When whispered voices cross the veil,
We stand between what was and what will be,
Honoring the past, embracing the unseen.
Spirits of old, kindred and wise,
Draw near, walk with us, bless this night.
We welcome you in love and light."

Calling the Sacred Fire

"O sacred fire, burning bright,
Guardian of the ancient rite,
Warm our souls, light our path,
Hold back the cold and winter's wrath.
As embers glow and shadows grow,
May wisdom spark and knowledge flow."

Invocation to the Ancestors

"Ancestors of blood and bone,
Ancestors of land and stone,
We honor you, we call your names,
Through memory's fire, your light remains.
Guide our steps, whisper clear,
We welcome you—be with us here."

Blessing of the Offerings

"Milk and honey, fruit and grain,
The gifts of life, the gifts of pain.
We lay these down with open hearts,
A token of love as the old year departs.
Spirits and kindred, accept our grace,
And bless us as we take our place."

The Passing of the Old Year

"The wheel has turned, the time is here,
To bid farewell to this passing year.
What must be left, we now release,
Ashes to wind, may we find peace.
Old regrets and shadows fade,
By fire's light, a new path is made."

Honoring the Dark and the Crone

"O Wise One, Cloaked in Night,
Keeper of secrets, Weaver of fate,
Teach us the strength of letting go,
The power of roots beneath the snow.
By your wisdom, we walk unafraid,
Embracing the lessons the darkness has made."

A Prayer for Protection Through the Dark

"O spirits, guides, and watchful kin,
Shield this space as night draws in.
May light within us brightly burn,
Until the sun and warmth return.
By oak, by stone, by fire's glow,
Safe we stand, let our courage grow."

Divination Invocation: Seeking the Future

"By flame, by bone, by sacred space,
Reveal to us what lies in place.
Visions of paths both dark and bright,
Guide our steps through this winter night.
O spirits of wisdom, answer our plea,
Show us the truths we are meant to see."

Closing the Veil: Farewell to the Spirits

"Kindred spirits, guides of old,
You've walked with us in the fire's hold.
With love we part, but not in sorrow,
We'll meet again in each tomorrow.
Go in peace, return in grace,
Until we gather in this sacred place."

Final Blessing: Embracing the Dark Half of the Year

"The wheel now turns, the light grows dim,
But wisdom shines from deep within.
Through winter's hush and starry sky,
The fire of life shall never die.
We walk in shadow, we walk in light,
Blessed be this Samhain night."

Printed in Great Britain
by Amazon